Buster's Christmas Letter

Buster's Christmas Letter

Lessons From a Dog's
Tale of Survival

by

ROBERT LEE WILSON

PARIBUS PUBLISHING, LTD
Irvington, New York

Published by
Paribus Publishing Ltd.
44 West Clinton Avenue, Irvington, NY 10533
www.ParibusPress.com

℗

Buster's Christmas Letter
Copyright © 2007 by Robert Lee Wilson
www.ParibusPress.com

FIRST EDITION

ISBN10: 1-933705-09-4
ISBN13: 978-1-933705-09-5

Printed in the United States of America

For Buster and Deb

Contents

Preface

I t has been an interesting year, which is a nice way of
saying the year has been difficult with an uncommon
string of bad luck. Stress is painful, but adversity has a way
of bringing out the best in people and, as I have come to
understand, in pets. So in this regard, it's been a very good year.
Each member of our family, including Buster, and numerous people
in our community stepped up to the challenges as circumstances
demanded.

The ordeal of Buster's survival helped us appreciate his
emotional connection to our family and his special gift of
unconditional love. The most amazing thing to me was that even
as he faced pain and possible death, he demonstrated the capacity
to empathize with us.

Each traumatic event generated an outpouring of kindness
from the community that reinforced my convictions. Despite all
the horrors of today's world, there are still plenty of
compassionate people. Their continued support sustains and
nurtures us in an increasingly competitive and material world.
Sometimes we just need to be reminded of their presence.

The warmth of the responses we received as we told our story gave me a sense that it could have a broad appeal. This book is my attempt to capture and share Buster's story as a way of saying thanks to all those who did so much to support my family.

My wife Deb kept telling me to write it down. "Just do it," she said. So I embarked on a disciplined process of writing this story. The more recent actions and chronology flowed easily, but my memory turned out to be fuzzier than I anticipated as I went back in time. More importantly, when I tried to capture everyone's emotions, I realized that I had significant gaps. Fortunately, my family took the time to fill in the actions and feelings that I had forgotten or misinterpreted. I appreciate their kind and loving support. Our collective memories have strengthened the truth and breadth of this story.

As work progressed, I started to connect the emotions and family roles like the pieces of a jigsaw puzzle. Buster's relationship with each of us was different and evolved over time. Initially, I found comfort in his role as protector of my young family and more recently was gratified to return the favor when his survival was at stake.

Contemplating this mosaic has given me a more profound sense of our feelings for Buster as individuals and collectively as a family. I have always known that people are quite attached to their pets, but I don't believe I understood the depth and complexity of those emotions until I looked at it from this perspective.

Deb frequently reminds me that "feelings are more important than things." How we feel about each other is essential to life, while material possessions or experiences, the things we have or do, are secondary. Being one who has always been more reserved about discussing emotions, I never fully appreciated her point until I experienced the events of the past year.

Deb and I are so much alike and yet quite different. I suppose that is why we make an enduring couple. We both enjoy the humor in everyday life and see the world in similar ways. But I tend to be more project and results oriented, while she feels more of the emotions from the twists and turns of life.

Christmas stirs powerful sentiments in many people and especially in me. The season is filled with family traditions, and one of my favorites is sending and receiving Christmas cards. Each card we receive rekindles fond memories and keeps us connected to dear friends whom we rarely see nowadays. Writing the letter we send with our cards is one of my favorite holiday activities because it allows me to relive and savor family activities of the past year.

So Deb was shocked this year when I shared my idea to have the family Christmas letter come from Buster. The idea, she thought, was a little too edgy, until she saw that I was motivated by feelings rather than by the humor or novelty of a dog writing a letter. The letter we sent touched many people intensely and brought this story into focus for me. Deb suggested that I include his letter in this book, and *Buster's Christmas Letter* has become both the title and theme of the story.

Pets play invaluable roles in our lives. They make us laugh, play with us, and are always there when we need companionship. The time we spend taking care of them makes them very special members of our families and builds enduring bonds. The benefits we receive are in proportion to the time we give. Getting a puppy is like the birth of a new baby. And yet the shorter lives of pets allow us to understand the importance of dignity in the aging process and the inevitability of death. Above all is the sense of wonder and joy pets bring into our lives, particularly during the holiday season.

I hope that you enjoy *Buster's Christmas Letter*, take his lessons to heart, and express your feelings and passion for life every day.

Lee Wilson
December 22, 2006

Buster's Christmas Letter

Family Addition

*M*y wife Deb and I moved to Milwaukee, Wisconsin, in 1987 because I was taking a new job. Neither of us was a native of Wisconsin, but we liked living in Milwaukee and believed it was a great place to raise a family. The city was large enough to have lots of interesting activities and yet small enough to make them readily accessible. Most important, we believed the city promoted strong family values consistent with our Midwest roots.

Deb was raised in Davenport, Iowa, as the third of six children in the boisterous Riefe family that owns and operates a restaurant bearing her family name. It serves the best fried chicken and pork tenderloins I have ever eaten and features a hamburger called the "Crazy Burger." Deb, her siblings and several of their children, her grandfather, her father, and her mother have worked in the business over the years.

I grew up in Quincy, Illinois, a small town on the Mississippi River with a rich history. One of the Lincoln-Douglas debates was held in Quincy. My grandfather was the mayor in the 1930s and later established a hardware store in town with my father. My grandfather, grandmother, father, and I all worked in the store. I came from a smaller and quieter family than Deb and have one older sister.

Deb and I met at DePauw, a small liberal arts college in Greencastle, Indiana. An attractive brunette of medium height with a slim build that reflected her training as a gymnast, she caught my attention early on. Her outgoing personality, love of laughter, and empathy gathered a wide circle of friends. We were married two years after graduation.

By 1990, Deb and I had started a family and were living with our three children and no pets in a house with a big yard in Milwaukee. Our hectic lives revolved around our children and their activities. Every day was an adventure, and life was good. Katie was seven, loved dolls, and was already becoming an avid reader. Robert was four and looking for mischief to avoid doing what Deb and Katie wanted him to do. James had just been born and was very cute with bright blue eyes but almost no hair.

The Wilson family was complete and contented with one significant exception: Katie and Robert desperately wanted a dog. Our good friends and neighbors, Lori and Bruce, had a dog named Buddy. He was a strikingly beautiful Australian shepherd with a wonderful, family-oriented disposition. Our entire family knew and adored Buddy. In addition, Katie was reading a series of books by Beverly Cleary, which featured a dog named Ribsy. And I suspect that Robert was looking for a pal in the family who would do what he wanted. The bottom line was that our children wanted a dog in the worst way.

They started working on us the way a starfish opens a scallop. The starfish is no match for the initial strength of a scallop, but the starfish applies steady pressure for long enough that the scallop eventually tires and succumbs. Few children are aware of the battles between starfish and scallops, but most are masters of this technique.

Deb kept them at bay for a while with the tried and true response, "I need to talk to your father." We weren't sure we had enough energy to handle a pet at the time and ultimately rationalized our decision to the children. "It would not be safe to have a dog with a new baby." So Katie and Robert wanted to know when James would be old enough, and that was when we committed our irretrievable error. We concluded, "You can have a dog when James is three years old."

My mother always told me, "Never promise something you don't intend to do." Moms are invariably right. At the time, James's third birthday seemed far away in the distant future, and we hoped that the children would forget the matter.

But children have an amazing way of remembering your promises, even if they sometimes forget their own. So on James's third birthday, Katie and Robert beseeched us, "Are we getting our dog today?" A promise was a promise, and we had to deliver on our word.

The first decision was selecting the type of dog best suited to our family. Although both Deb and I had grown up with dogs, we soon learned that we had incompatible views on the matter. My father has always been an outdoorsman, and over the years my family had two Irish setters and then an English setter. Patty, George, and Gatsby lived outside and were more my dad's hunting dogs than pets for my sister and me. The notion of an outside dog was deeply embedded in my childhood memories, and that was what I had in mind for my family.

Deb had an entirely different concept in mind. She had grown up with a Norwegian elkhound named Nina, a family pet for the children. Deb dreamed of having an inside family dog like Nina, but she was flexible on the breed. Deb had always wanted a Samoyed, a beautiful, white dog similar to a husky. But recently, she had begun to favor golden retrievers, handsome animals with calmer dispositions around children.

The matter was settled for us when Lori and Bruce announced the arrival of a new litter of puppies from the same lineage as their dog Buddy. Several of our friends were going to select puppies from this litter, and we had an immediate family consensus to pursue the opportunity. Of course, Buddy was an inside dog, so Deb was going to have her way.

According to the book *Australian Shepherds* by Joseph Hartnagle,[1] "Aussies, as the dogs are commonly known, are not originally from Australia as you might suppose." The breed started in the Basque region between Spain and France and was exported to Australia because of its superior characteristics as a shepherd. The dogs became known as Australian shepherds when they were introduced to the United States in the early 1900s along with flocks of imported sheep from down under.[2]

There are three main varieties of Aussies. Red merles have copper and white fur, blue merles have gray and white fur, and tricolors have copper, gray, and black spots. Their markings can come in many combinations, so each dog is unique.

According to Hartnagle, "These dogs were renowned throughout the sheep country for their keen herding ability, protective nature, and intense devotion to their master." Because Aussies have interesting personalities, it is not surprising that

---

[1] Jospeh Hartnagle, *Australian Shepherds*, Neptune City, NJ, TFH Publications, March 1995.
[2] Ibid., 6.

they were featured in two Disney movies: *Stubby, the World's Greatest Cowdog* and *Run, Appaloosa, Run.*[3]

Choosing our dog, the newest member of our family, was a momentous decision. But at that juncture, I wasn't sure how much my opinion mattered. I assumed that the primary decision had been made when we selected the breed and lineage. How we would choose the specific dog was an issue I hadn't given much thought. We would somehow just know what to do when we got to that point.

On the appointed day, Deb and I drove several miles to see the puppies and select our dog. Neither of us remembers why we didn't take the children, but I'm certain the decision was easier with two opinions rather than five. We rang the doorbell of a nice country house at the proper address and were met by a pleasant woman who said we had come to the right place. She showed us into a bedroom where the litter of puppies was squirming around in a large cardboard box.

After admiring the puppies for a while, Deb started to narrow the choices. "What do you think about this one?" she asked. "No, I think maybe this one is prettier." Then after pausing a moment and still unable to decide, she groaned "Oh, I don't know, What do you think?"

Diplomatically I responded, "There are lots of nice puppies, but I really like the two your prefer."

With that, she decided, "I think this one is the best." A male tricolor, the puppy had interesting markings that I thought would make him a handsome dog. He was the smallest and quietest of the litter.

---

[3] Ibid., 8-9

I remember holding him for the first time. He was small enough to fit in the palm of my hand, and his eyes were still shut. He was cute as he wiggled around, and I felt like I was holding one of my own newborn children in the hospital. I had a father's sense of pride and expectation.

In reality, assessing a dog's personality at that early stage is difficult—just as difficult as anticipating the character of your newborn child. But when my friend Walter saw my son James at a few weeks of age, he correctly noted that James seemed unusually sensitive to those around him. I've always wondered if Deb had Walter's ability to sense something special, which attracted her to our dog. In retrospect, knowing the other dogs from the litter, her choice was clearly the best match for our family, but not in the ways I would have suspected.

As we drove home, the look on Deb's face told me that she was not certain about her decision.

She asked, "Do you think we made the right choice?"

After a pause to think about it, I answered confidently, "Yes, I think he'll be great."

Not fully convinced, she queried, "Are you sure?"

A little exasperated, I replied, "I wouldn't have said so if I didn't mean it." Over the years, I have come to appreciate that Deb wants validation of her decisions, but at the time I wasn't sure why we needed further discussion of a case I considered to be closed.

The next big decision was what to name our dog. Deb purchased an advice book on naming dogs so we could do it properly. She and the children had lots of fun exploring the possibilities. As they sat around the kitchen table, Deb read aloud the list of the most popular names and what each indicated about a dog's personality. Katie and Robert would say "I like that one" or "No way." After several hours, they finally settled on "Buster" and told me their choice after I got home from work.

Personally, I had never dreamed of naming a dog Buster. It wasn't that I had anything against that name in particular; it's just that no one I knew had ever named a dog Buster. Yet knowing my place as a good husband and father, I bit my tongue and accepted their decision. I was resigned to having an inside dog named Buster. Although it turned out to be a great name that fit his lovable, exuberant personality, this was not apparent to me at the time.

Six weeks later, when the puppies were old enough to leave their mother, we drove out to the breeder to pick up Buster. At first sight, Deb pronounced him adorable. He had a hint of copper on his face and two blue eyes, one of which changed to brown as he grew older. The children were jubilant because they had anticipated this day for so long. We were adding a new member to our family.

Revelations

*D*eb held Buster on her lap as we drove home. I looked over at her, and as I caught her eye, she started to cry. I was touched that she was being sentimental about the moment. Only that evening did I learn how mistaken I had been. Apparently, the realization had suddenly hit her that she wasn't going to get a golden retriever—at least not anytime soon. She was taking on the primary care and responsibility for a dog with a fourteen-year life expectancy and was having second thoughts. But there was no turning back at that point.

About half way home, Deb started to sneeze. Her eyes began to itch, and by the time we turned into our driveway, she was suffering what appeared to be an attack of hay fever. I suggested she wash her hands and face, and that seemed to help. But her suffering continued, so she started to take antihistamines for relief until whatever pollen was causing her problem subsided.

The mystery of Deb's allergic reaction was solved a few days later when I was playing with Buster. I noticed that my eyes were starting to itch. I'm allergic to lots of things and had been tested extensively, but dogs were not previously identified as a problem. Yet allergies often develop over time. I hurried into the kitchen and laughed to Deb, "You're not going to believe this, but we're allergic to Buster."

She exclaimed, "You can't be serious!"

But with a combination of resignation and conviction, I replied, "I hate to say it, Deb, but I'm certain that Buster is the problem."

Through a process of trial and error over the next week, we confirmed that both Deb and I were severely allergic to Buster. The longer he was in our house, the more our eyes watered, and Deb would sometimes get welts on her skin. We sneezed every time we touched him, and antihistamines were no match for this dog's dandruff. Our only sure defense was to leave the house, and the next-best alternative was to constantly wash our hands and faces.

Some might be surprised that we never had a discussion about whether we should keep Buster. I'm sure Deb had her initial doubts, and I certainly had mine as I contemplated the years of misery to come. But we never voiced any thoughts about getting rid of him. By the time we fully comprehended the issue; we were too attached to this lovable ball of fur and couldn't bear to return him. We were just going to have to figure it out.

So we turned our attention to housebreaking Buster. This process could take several months, so at first he slept in our basement. He appeared to like it there and began converting our downstairs playroom into his home. But he had to go to the bathroom frequently, and he did so wherever he pleased. Not being used to having an inside dog, I didn't realize that once he had gone to the bathroom in a particular spot, it was marked for future use by the odor. The advantage of having a concrete floor in our basement was that I could squirt some liquid soap on the spot and hose it down rather than scrub it clean on my hands and knees. My nose is sensitive to odors, and just the thought of cleaning dog accidents made me gag. I had never heard of a product called Nature's Miracle before we got Buster. It claimed to remove any trace of smell so the dog would not return to the spot. But that proved irrelevant with Buster, who was always looking for virgin territory. By December, he was housebroken, but I was already far too near the end of my rope and ready for Christmas to lift my spirits.

Buster had only been with us for about three months when our next surprise was how destructive a pet could be. One evening, I went down to the basement, where Buster slept, after hearing him scratching at the door. When I opened it, I saw to my horror numerous vertical gouges in the wood just below the knob. I couldn't imagine that such a small puppy could cause that much damage so quickly. How was I going to fix this? "Bad dog, bad dog!" I scolded Buster as I held his paw to the door. But given my emerging experience with him, I realized that this probably would have little effect.

This episode was followed within two weeks by my revelation that chewing by dogs inside a house can quickly destroy furniture, furniture I had purchased with my hard-earned paychecks. Deb and I had agonized over finding the right couch for the family room; she favors colors and style, while my ability to like a piece of furniture is directly proportional to my ability to afford it. It was a Saturday morning, and I had just come in from shoveling snow off the steps. As I worked, I had contemplated how to deal with Buster's destructive behavior. I walked into the house and discovered him gnawing a large hole in one of the couch cushions. I grabbed the cushion, but he would not let go. I repeated words that were becoming all too familiar: "Bad dog, bad dog." Finally, I managed to pry his jaws apart and replaced the cushion, turning the ruined side to the back. I know that dogs love to chew, but outside dogs chew things like sticks and rocks, which don't cost anything. I wondered, why couldn't Buster be like that?

The final straw for me was the dirt and hair that began to accumulate throughout the house. Even Deb was beginning to grouse about it.

I got into bed one evening and announced, "I think it's time for Buster to become an outside dog."

Deb defended him, answering, "I know he's not perfect, but he's getting better."

I persisted. "We're both allergic to him, and he's destroying our house. He has to live outside."

She whimpered, "But it's cold and dark outside at night. He'll be frightened."

It seemed obvious to me that a dog bred for herding sheep on the range was quite well suited to living outdoors. But I compromised, suggesting, "He can stay in the basement at night and be outside during the day. But he can't have the run of our house."

"I suppose you're right. Let's see how it works," she responded, signaling her partial acceptance, and so at seven months old, Buster was to become a mostly outdoor dog.

Implementing my plan was more complex than simply putting him out in the yard. Teaching a dog to stay on your property and not run astray takes a while. With Buster, it might take a while longer. I strung a long wire between two trees in our backyard and bought a collar and chain that, when hooked to the wire, let him run back and forth. I thought it was a practical solution, but it was soon clear that he hated being constrained, so the children let him loose to play whenever they could.

Training Buster turned out to be even harder than I expected. Discipline clearly was not a word in Buster's vocabulary. We must have spent hundreds of dollars on the endeavor. He had lessons with trainers by himself, with the children, and with Deb and me. We even sent him to a sleep-away camp, but to no avail.

I can still feel the exasperation and hopelessness. I can picture Buster standing there in front of me as I tell him to sit. I would try to help him by pressing down on his hindquarters. But he would cock his head and jump up on me. He may have picked up something from all his training, but the results were not apparent at the time.

One day in June, Deb took Katie and Robert over for a swim at our neighbor's new pool. Buster was very excited and ran way too fast toward Katie. He slipped on a puddle of water and skidded into the pool. Having never been in the water, he was surprised and, for a moment, panicked. Fearing that Buster would not know how to swim, Deb impulsively leaped in fully clothed and rescued him.

The sight of the pair was comical. Buster's fluffy fur normally made him appear much larger, but with it matted to his body, he looked skinny and half the size. With her drenched dress clinging to her body and her hair askew, Deb looked like Lucy Ricardo on *I Love Lucy* after getting herself into another predicament. Everyone got a chuckle out of that one, and Deb was thankful no cameras were around.

Another humorous situation that summer taught Buster a lesson he did manage to retain. Buster enjoyed being outdoors, and we rapidly learned how much he loved to run and chase things. Most of all, he adored chasing squirrels. He had never caught one, but he came darn close several times. While Buster was still a young dog, a baby deer found its way into our backyard. Buster had never seen a "squirrel" so big and took off after the fawn. He disappeared, chasing it into the woods behind our house, and we wondered what was going to happen next. Then we heard a blood-curdling yelp as Buster raced out of the woods, chased by the fawn's mother. She was on a protective mission, and Buster was the enemy. He realized that she was big and meant business, so he was running for his life. She followed him nearly halfway across the yard and then stopped. He scampered all the way back to the house and hid in the garage. While he still barked at deer, I never saw him chase one again.

There was another incident earlier in his life that had a huge impact on Buster. Sometimes childhood traumas establish fears that last a lifetime. Such was the case with Buster and lightning. Aussies have very fine fur that makes them ultrasensitive to electrical storms and predisposes this fear. Late in March, just after he became a mostly outdoor dog, there was a terrible thunderstorm in Milwaukee. We were having dinner at a restaurant with the children that evening, and Buster was home alone. As the storm howled outside, a downspout became clogged, and water flooded a section of the basement near his bed. Lightning struck our house, knocking down a section of the chimney and taking out the electric power. We returned to a darkened house to find Buster huddled in a corner and shaking. I can only imagine how frightened he must have been. After that night, just the slightest rumble of thunder in the distance caused him to panic.

Despite his somewhat inauspicious start with our family, the most important thing was that the children quickly came to love Buster. Deb took him on walks with her friends and their dogs. These walks were therapeutic for her and helped Buster get rid of his excess energy. Over time, the walks launched what became an enduring, loving relationship. I enjoyed the way the children and I played with Buster, but I had to pay for all the things he destroyed. The amount we paid the breeder to get Buster was just the tip of the iceberg in terms of his total cost. He was a high-maintenance dog. So I had more of a love-hate relationship with Buster. It would take a little longer for him to win me over completely.

Moving

*L*ess than a year after Buster joined our family, my job took me to New York. We knew this would be difficult for the children, so we waited until we were on vacation in Florida to break the news to Katie and Robert. Deb told Katie, who responded with tears, while I told Robert, who simply refused to accept the situation. After an hour of separately walking the beach and golf course, Katie and Robert accepted the inevitable, but they were very unhappy about leaving their friends. We assumed that James was young enough to simply go along with the program, but to this day he complains about being taken for granted. Deb and I were not excited about the prospects of uprooting our family and leaving such a wonderful place to raise our children.

Worse than that, we weren't sure if taking Buster with us was such a good idea. We had a big yard for an outside dog in Wisconsin, but would that be available in suburban Connecticut? Perhaps he would be better off with a good home in Milwaukee. But how could we bear to leave him?

Deb consulted our veterinarian, Dr. David Rosene. He gave us sound advice. He explained, "Taking Buster will provide important continuity in your lives and help the transition to a new home. No matter how sad the children are, they will always have Buster to console them." His wisdom settled the issue, and we decided that Buster was moving with us.

Transporting a dog like Buster from Wisconsin was no small feat. The moving van was taking our furniture, and we were flying to New York. Buster couldn't go on the truck and had become much too large to fit under my seat on the airplane. We couldn't drive him to New York because of work and school schedules, so what could we do?

As usual, Deb gathered information and discovered that Buster could fly with the baggage on our plane. She went shopping for the necessary equipment, and a man at the pet store sold her a helpful contraption. It was a collapsible cage that easily could be reused after the flight and was, therefore, well worth the somewhat-steep price. Deb studied literature from the airline about the importance of keeping your pet properly hydrated and nourished in transit and ultimately chose not to give him tranquilizers as some people do. We followed all the instructions carefully and even gave Buster a final drink of water at the airport.

After bidding a tearful good-bye, we checked in and headed for our plane. The flight to New York boarded quickly, but the two-hour journey seemed to take forever. I was feeling guilty, thinking about poor Buster in the plane's dark cargo hold, wondering what he thought was happening to him. We arrived in New York and waited anxiously at the baggage claim. As each bag came out and Buster was not there, we became more nervous. "When will he be here?" the children kept asking.

Finally, we inquired about Buster and learned that there was a special area for pet collection. After we found him, we were greatly relieved as he bounded out of his cage rambunctious as ever and seemingly none the worse for the wear. Although the high-priced cage had served its purpose well, we never used it again, and I gave it away ten years later when we were cleaning out the garage.

Shortly after arriving in Connecticut, we established one of the first rituals in our new home: celebrating Buster's birthday. It's funny, but I don't think I ever knew the birthday of any family pet, and yet Deb claims that everyone knows their pets' birthdays. Katie loves traditions and remembered that Buster's birthday was August 24th, so we decided to have a party. (To Deb's chagrin, the way Katie continues to remember her mom's birthday is that it's exactly one month from Buster's.)

Deb made a birthday cake and placed it on a small table that we had set up in the yard. I lit the candle, and we all sang "Happy Birthday" to Buster. He struggled as I held him back for fear the candle might catch his fur on fire. Deb cut a slice for Buster and gave it to him on a birthday-themed paper plate. She cautioned the children to eat slowly and chew their food, but Buster was having none of that. He inhaled his piece and looked like he was getting ready to pounce on the rest. Deb moved the cake to a safer location, and to our amusement he started to lick and chew his paper plate. The children laughed, thinking this was great fun. Later, Katie and Robert helped Buster unwrap his presents, and his favorite was a dried pig's ear, which he enjoyed gnawing immensely.

Then it was time for his big birthday present. We took him around the house and proudly showed him his new dwelling place. This was no ordinary doghouse. Deb and I had gone down to the local pet warehouse and selected one constructed of wood with asphalt shingles on the roof. It was a little expensive, but this was his new home. I purchased some carpet to put on the floor to make it softer and warmer. I thought it was just right for an outdoor dog.

We all watched anxiously as Buster looked at his new doghouse. He went up and stared at it and then backed away. I coaxed him to stick his head in, and he sniffed it, but he turned around and ran off. It was perfect in every respect except one: Buster hated his new doghouse. He refused to go inside and would have nothing to do with it.

We tried putting food in it, and he simply stuck his head in, grabbed the food, and carried it into the yard to eat it. To make matters worse, he continuously pulled the carpet out of it, as if to say, "I hate this place."

Robert is always coming up with creative solutions, so one day he decided to climb inside the doghouse and coax Buster to join him. That it worked was both the good news and the bad news. Once Buster wedged his way inside with Robert, the quarters were too cramped for him to turn around or back his way out the door. Robert yelled for help, and eventually Katie heard him and got Deb. Together, they managed to get Buster's hind legs out the door and free the two of them. That was the end of Buster's doghouse and the start of a lifelong case of claustrophobia for Robert.

We tried to return the doghouse, but the pet warehouse manager said all sales were final. We eventually managed to give it to some friends. I'll never forget how happy I was to see June and Eric drive away with it in the trunk of their car. They never mentioned whether their dog liked it, and I was afraid to ask, for fear they would want to return it. But once the doghouse was gone, we decided that Buster should continue to sleep in our garage on a permanent basis.

The only thing missing was a plan to keep Buster in our yard during the day without a chain. This was resolved by a marvelous invention we discovered in Connecticut called Invisible Fence. A wire buried in the ground transmits a signal that is picked up by a collar worn by the dog. When the dog gets within six feet of the wire, the collar starts its warning beeps. The closer the pet comes, the faster the beeping. When the animal gets directly over the wire, or "invisible fence," the two metal prongs on the inside of the collar give the pooch an electric shock.

Now, this may sound cruel, but the installation cost includes training and temporary warning flags to alert the dog. After just one or two shocks, the dog is completely trained. Despite his earlier lack of discipline, Buster proved a quick study, and he now had the complete run of our yard without any other constraint. He was free to chase squirrels, bark at strangers, or take a nap wherever he pleased.

However, the Invisible Fence was not without its mishaps. Buster would sometimes escape from our yard when he panicked during an electric storm or when he was chasing a car so fast that he didn't have time to stop.

Sometimes it wasn't his fault. One of the few things Buster liked as much as food was going for a ride in the car. I suppose this was because he went for a ride when Deb took him to walk with her friends and their dogs. All you had to do was open the back of the minivan, and he jumped in immediately. We were always careful to remove his collar whenever taking him for a ride. But when the fence was new, both Deb and I managed to forget to remove Buster's collar. You can imagine our feelings of guilt as we drove away and heard the beep and then a yelp from the back of the vehicle. Neither of us ever made that mistake twice, at least that we admitted.

Buster settled into his life in Connecticut taking walks with Deb, playing with the children, "helping" me as I worked in the yard, and ruling his roost. He became an important member of our family and helped smooth the transition for all of us in our new home. We knew he was smart, friendly, and good looking. Our pride in Buster was reinforced each time we took him someplace as other people seemed to notice and like him. They would ask what breed he was, because not that many people were familiar with Australian shepherds. So it was fun to answer questions and tell people about him.

The opportunity to confirm our belief that Buster was a superior creature came the next year when Katie was twelve. We received a flyer in the mail for a local dog show called "Putting on the Dog." Katie is an achiever like many first children, so competing in a dog show came to her naturally. Now this was a fun show—not as competitive as the famous Westminster Dog Show in New York City—but it was sponsored by a worthy organization and was a good start for Buster, who was almost two.

After school, when Katie found the flyer sitting with the mail on the kitchen table, she studied it and exclaimed to Deb, "Look, there's a dog show, and I think we should enter Buster. He could win."

Deb was intrigued and asked, "But who is going to groom him and handle him at the show?"

"I can do it." Katie beamed with pride, which melted Deb's heart and objections. So it was decided between them that Buster should enter the competition, and when the rest of us heard the news, we were excited and quite certain he would win.

Katie practiced with Buster in the yard, getting him to heel and sit on her command, and I was impressed with his progress. Deb had Buster groomed at the kennel, and Katie brushed his fur in final preparation. On the day of the show, the whole family took Buster with great expectations.

I started to worry when I studied the categories and learned that the competition was by size rather than breed. When the judge finally arrived, he asked what breed Buster was, which seemed a little odd coming from someone who was supposed to be an expert. Katie told him that Buster was an Australian shepherd, to which he remarked that he had heard that "an Aussie's temperament makes it a poor family dog." That comment really got Deb's dander up, but she bit her tongue, not wanting to make him mad at us. Unfortunately, this prejudice was the extent of his "knowledge" about Aussies, so he had no way of knowing whether Buster was a good or bad example of his kind.

To make matters worse, when the owners were asked to walk their dogs, Buster's lack of discipline reasserted itself. He proved far more interested in checking out the other canines than in following Katie's instructions, and she felt stressed and embarrassed trying to make him behave.

Although he was the prettiest dog in his size category, he did not win, place, or show. Buster didn't even win the costume competition, for which the children had dressed him in a hilarious outfit as a beach bum using my swimsuit and sunglasses. Deb was surprised that I never wore that swimsuit again. She said that she washed it, but I was trained by my mother never to wear another person's swimsuit or underwear.

We returned home somewhat dejected, but consoled ourselves with complaints about the judge. Deb made a bowl of popcorn, which she assured us always makes every situation better. We all shared it as we sat around the kitchen table.

"He didn't know what he was doing," Robert groused.

Deb, still smarting from the judge's comment about Aussies not being family dogs, remarked, "He was just a crabby old man."

James, only five years old, added, "I think Buster knew the man didn't like him, but I don't think his feelings are hurt about not winning."

Always the optimist, Katie chimed in. "Well, there's always next year."

The following year, we took Buster back to the show, and he behaved much better. The new judge had heard of Australian shepherds, although the categories were still by size rather than breed, and Buster took only third place. We were convinced that he should have won first prize, and he was a winner as far as we were concerned. But we concluded that the categories were not suited to a dog of his obvious caliber, and that was the end of dog shows for Buster. I suspect that owners of other dogs who didn't win may have shared our sentiments.

Looking back on it now, around the time of the dog shows something seemed to strengthen the bond between Katie and Buster. It might have been Katie taking responsibility for the contest or discovering that he fit some need in her life during her middleschool years. Whatever the reason, when she came home after school, Katie spent extra time greeting Buster and gently scratching his back. One day, she confided to Deb, "Dogs make great friends because they are never unkind to you."

The connection between Deb and Buster was also being strengthened in Connecticut. Walks were the catalyst that accelerated the development of their relationship. Over the years, they took hundreds, if not thousands, of walks together. All the time they spent together made their bond so enduring.

Deb likes to walk for exercise, and so do several of her friends. It's natural for them to take their dogs on walks while catching up with one another.

When he was younger, Buster never seemed to get the concept of taking a walk. He was always so excited that he wanted to run and on several occasions nearly pulled Deb's arm out of its socket as she tried to slow him down. She couldn't bring herself to use one of those choke collars that tighten as the dog pulls, so she settled for a regular leash and a brisk pace. Eventually, age slowed Buster down, and by the time he was five, they settled into a routine of long, pleasant walks.

In later years, Buster developed arthritis, for which he took medicine. As he aged, his mobility declined. A twelve-year-old dog is not nearly as agile as a puppy. Jumping into the back of the minivan became more difficult, and lifting him was not easy. Deb saw an ad for a pet ramp in an airline magazine and bought it. This seemed like such a logical invention, but Buster absolutely refused to use it. I don't know whether he was too proud or he was afraid of falling off. As a result, Deb continued to lift him into the van.

The walks became less frequent in recent years, but that seemed to make them something they both relished even more. These walks with Buster are among her fondest memories. She told me that walking a dog is therapeutic. "You have the fresh air, a constant companion who is your best friend, and the exercise releases your stress. The responsibility to walk the dog is yours, but at the end of the day, you benefit from the routine." I'm thankful that Buster gave her this gift and a bit jealous that she referred to him as her best friend, but I'm relieved that she doesn't feel the need to grab a leash and take me for a walk…yet.

Mischief

*B*uster developed the annoying habit of digging and sleeping in my gardens after we moved to Connecticut. The pachysandra ground cover around the exterior of our house made a comfortable bed for his naps but were systematically destroyed by his intrusions. Each time I noticed a new area was ruined, my blood pressure went up a few notches. He particularly enjoyed lying in the garden that I had planted just outside our kitchen window. From there, he could watch over us and be part of the family. Perhaps lying on my flowers was his revenge for not being allowed to join us for dinner inside.

This was especially frustrating for me because gardening is one of my favorite hobbies. Some men are difficult to buy for, but selecting a gift for me is simple. I always need a new trowel, shovel, pair of gloves, or some other garden gadget.

I tried scolding him, but that didn't work. Next, I purchased some attractive ornamental fencing at the garden center, which was no deterrent at all, as he merely jumped over it.

Finally, after months of rising tension, I conceived a plan to thwart Buster's mischief in my gardens and put a halt to the destruction. If an Invisible Fence could keep a dog in, it could also be used to keep him out. So I called the folks at Canine Fence and asked them to come back. I explained my plan to run a loop next to the perimeter of the house through my gardens. There would be no Invisible Fence in front of the garage, because Buster would need access to sleep at night.

The two technicians who arrived at our house for the installation listened with amusement as I explained my scheme. They had seen every conceivable installation to keep a dog in, but they had never installed a fence to keep a dog out. My wife, who was going to be a math major in college before she switched to economics, enjoys reciting this story when she explains to friends that I am "several standard deviations from the norm."

My new plan worked, but Buster ended up having the last laugh. Outside our kitchen is a little hill planted with azalea, hydrangea, and spirea bushes that I had neglected to include in my design. Buster simply moved his perch to this new location and settled in. Although he was a little farther from the house, being atop the hill put him at eye level, and he enjoyed watching our every move.

The next summer, he dug a burrow under one of the spirea bushes to keep himself cool, and he learned to enjoy walking back and forth under the branches to scratch his back. I concluded that some aspects of a dog's behavior could not be controlled, and as long as this mischief was confined to one location, I would have to learn to live with it.

Deb had her own challenges with Buster. One day, she looked out the window and noticed that a delivery man was running around in our front yard. She realized he was chasing Buster but was clearly no match for his speed. The dog had something wrapped in brown paper in his mouth.

Deb ran out the door and entered the chase, which continued for a few minutes. Buster seemed to be toying with them by stopping, dropping the package, and then running away with it each time they came close. Finally, she managed to corner the dog and retrieve the package, which turned out to be a sack with the driver's lunch inside. She scolded Buster, who had managed to eat part of it. Then she apologized profusely to the man and reimbursed him for his sandwich.

There was nothing Buster enjoyed more in life than a meal he managed to steal. He was smart and knew exactly where to look for food. His keen sense of smell allowed him to zero in on potential delicacies, and his superior speed allowed him to strike at a moment's notice. What he seemed to crave, in order of priority, were meat, fat, and sweets—and he didn't mind a bit if he had to swallow a little tinfoil or cellophane to get them. Wouldn't you prefer a steak or a piece of pizza to a low-fat rice dinner?

Dogs sometimes chase deliverymen, but with Buster it was often the other way around. His most common pursuers were unsuspecting workers who came to our house. The plumber, the electrician, UPS drivers, and numerous others all fell prey to his cunning. Many of these people carried doughnuts or their lunch in a bag while they made their rounds. With a quick sniff, Buster knew if they had anything worth taking. The doors on many delivery trucks are open, and it was mere puppy play for Buster to jump in, grab the sack, and run away.

Sometimes the victim's food was left in a closed truck, and Buster distracted the person when he or she opened the vehicle door. He operated like a skilled pickpocket. Once the poor soul diverted his or her attention to pet Buster, the trap was set. Buster quickly jumped inside, grabbed the food, and bolted off before they knew what had hit them. I can't tell you exactly how many workers Deb reimbursed for stolen lunches over the years, but it's closer to a hundred than to ten.

Another technique Buster used in his quest for food was infiltrating our house when a visitor was there. At the doorway, Buster squeezed by the unsuspecting person's legs and raced in. Buster lived outside, but he enjoyed sneaking inside every chance he got because he knew he would find something to eat. Our family was quite familiar with this tactic, but a workman or guest had little chance against such a scheme. All it took was for the door between the garage and the house to be ajar for a moment, and Buster would sprint into the kitchen. Deb usually had some dessert on the counter, and he grabbed it in a flash. He could consume a considerable portion of pie or cake in the time it took for a normal person to catch up to him, and nobody liked to eat what is left on the floor.

We had a standing rule to warn any new person coming into our house about this ruse, but Buster's strength and speed continued to prevail. The container with his dog food was inside the house, right next to the garage door where he entered. Once inside, he could easily knock it over and have all the dog food he wanted, but as a clear sign of his discerning palate, this never happened.

Over the years, his most annoying trick was raiding the garbage. Inside the garage, the garbage cans were difficult to tip over, but outside they were easy marks—a buffet table for a dog. My theory on why Buster didn't like the garbage men is that he knew they were taking his free lunch.

I remember the first time this happened, not long after we moved to Connecticut in 1994. I was on my way to work and dressed in a suit. As I opened the garage door, I noticed garbage strewn all over the driveway. I saw Buster sitting on the lawn, contentedly chewing on what appeared to be a bone. I scolded him and started to pick up the mess, which had a terrible smell. It was slimy as I put it back in the can, and under my breath I was saying unkind words.

Then I attempted to get the bone away from Buster. I had to chase him for a couple of minutes, and when I finally caught him, he didn't willingly give up his loot. He nipped at my hand, and it hurt. I managed to get the bone from him, and I went back into the house to wash my hands and change my suit, which had gotten dirty. Fortunately, the wound on my hand was just a scratch. But it made painfully clear why his chart at the kennel had a bright red sticker to warn "Will bite."

In our quest for a solution, we tried every type of garbage can, and none of them were "Buster-proof." I don't know how he did it, but he even managed to open cans secured with bungee cords over the top. The only solution was to put out the garbage just before the pickup, which was not always practical with our schedules.

Food was obviously important to Buster, and I consistently spoiled him with table scraps. This was probably not good for him, and my corrupting influence undoubtedly contributed to his mischief. But I couldn't resist, and we both enjoyed it. He watched us eat dinner in the kitchen from his perch on the hill, and when the meal was over, I would take him some tempting morsels, like the fat I cut off my meat. I would stick my head out the door and entice him, calling, "I have something for you." He would run around the corner of the house to meet me in the garage and then sit attentively and wait for me to toss him the first piece. Buster was very adept at catching and immediately returned to his stance, awaiting the next bite. I dropped the pieces from above his head, which experience showed was far safer than letting him bite them while they were in my hand. He would get too excited, and I had other good uses for my fingers. Once the food was gone, I would linger a while and scratch his ears and tell him he was a good dog. Over time, this feeding routine solidified our friendship, which once was in doubt.

King

*B*uster was clearly the king of his realm. Although his range was circumscribed by the Invisible Fence, he fiercely defended his turf and subjects. It may not have been the biggest dog kingdom in town, but it was his kingdom. Each morning, he surveyed his territory, barking at every living thing to announce that he had arrived and was very much in charge.

Every kingdom faces the risk of invasion from some mortal enemy. Despite his vigilance, Buster's regal borders were not impervious, especially to aerial attacks. Birds were one of Buster's biggest challenges. The cause of the conflict was initially a battle for food, and the antagonists were principally crows and blue jays.

We put his food and water dishes outside the garage so he could indulge himself whenever he was hungry or thirsty. This proved far too tempting for the birds. They would sit in nearby trees, waiting for him to go to another part of the yard or, better yet, to fall asleep. Then they would swoop down on his food dish, grab a nugget of his dried dog food, and fly back into the trees to enjoy it at their leisure.

Like many kings, Buster only liked stealing when he was the thief. Seeing the birds stealing his own food drove him crazy. If he came around the house while a bird was at his dish, he would run at it as fast as he could. The message of his bark was unmistakably clear: "Leave my food alone." But as many times as I saw him chase the birds, he never came close to catching one. The greatest indignity was the way the birds would sit up in the trees afterward and taunt him with their calls while they devoured their stolen treasure.

After four or five years when we bought a new dog feeder, his food was moved inside the garage, and the battle was over. But even in his old age, whenever he saw birds sitting in the trees near the garage, he raced to the scene and barked at them.

Deer were the largest intruders in Buster's kingdom. They are beautiful creatures, but they're a gardener's nightmare, and they spread ticks carrying Lyme disease. When he was younger, Buster often refused to come inside on a cold, snowy night, sensing that the enemy was just beyond the shadows. Deer are nocturnal grazers, and sometimes in the middle of the night, Deb would hear Buster barking, and she would wake me to bring him in before he bothered the neighbors.

As he got older, Buster's defenses became more relaxed, and I relied more on netting, fences, and sprays to thwart the deer.

Robert was always the best at checking Buster for ticks. I think he was particularly sensitive to the danger because of all the backpacking trips he has taken. While petting Buster, he would feel for a large bump—a tick—on his skin. For several summers, we diligently found and removed these tiny, dangerous pests. We knew to be careful not to pull off the body engorged with blood, as this would leave the infected head embedded in his skin.

Fortunately, not every tick is infected, but Buster once tested positive for Lyme disease and required a four-week course of antibiotics.

A better technique for removing ticks is to touch the hot end of a match that has just been blown out to the back of a tick. The tick will disengage, allowing you to safely remove it. However, the odds of success for this procedure on people are far better than on a large, squirming dog. Eventually, we found that regular spraying of the yard for ticks was better protection for Buster and ourselves.

A king needs leisure to balance his duties defending his realm. Chasing squirrels appeared to be the sport of choice for our king. I never witnessed any transgression that should have elicited the fervor of Buster's chase whenever one of these furry creatures chanced to cross his path. He simply loved to chase squirrels, and it was good exercise for him.

We often joked about Buster's sport, wondering what he would do if he ever caught one. Squirrels are fast and have the advantage of being able to climb trees to escape. But they're not invincible, and some are smarter and quicker than others, as unfortunate roadkill clearly attests. Only once, when he was three years old, did he ever temporarily catch a squirrel. Buster was so surprised that he loosened his bite momentarily, and the panicked squirrel managed to escape.

The most common visitors to his kingdom were people, usually in cars or trucks. Buster was there in a flash, wanting to sniff and jump up on the unsuspecting people the moment they opened their doors. He was generally friendly, simply trying to say hello. However, he did not understand or follow our human conventions for personal space and appropriate zones for touching. Most dog owners understand instinctively, but others are frequently shocked. Everyone in our family knew to be on duty to restrain him from being too friendly when someone came to visit.

Most of the time, he determined that the person was just fine, but there were a few people over the years whom he did not like, and you could tell it immediately. He didn't attack, but the sound of his bark said that he might, if provoked. Perhaps he sensed they didn't like him, or—in the case of the garbage man—he was protecting his potential source of food. Deb had a more generous theory about the garbage man, claiming that Buster was protecting us from a person taking something from our house. But I've got my story, and I'm sticking to it.

Our monarch was a shepherd and a herder by instinct. When a car or truck started to leave our driveway, he herded it down the road, chasing it and nipping at the tires. This always made us nervous, because one of his relatives back in Wisconsin was killed when he got too close to a car doing the same thing.

Buster used to herd our children when they were younger. He would nudge them with his head when they were running. The kids thought it was funny, but Robert didn't care for it when Buster nipped at his feet while he was riding his bike. We would sometimes have to put Buster in the garage when other children came over to play. Although he wasn't trying to be unfriendly, Buster's size and energy could sometimes be frightening to a small child.

Robert came up with a practical solution for such situations. If he and James had friends over to play basketball, Buster would often want to join in the action, and that could spoil the game. Robert would open the back of the minivan, and Buster would hop right in, supposing he was going for a ride. That was the end of the annoyance.

The first time this happened, I remember wondering where Buster was that evening. I was worried that he might have gotten out of the yard. I asked Robert if he had seen him, and he said, "Oops. I forgot. I put him in the back of the minivan because he was ruining our game." We went outside and found him quite content to be resting in the trunk. But I admonished Robert to be careful on a warm day to let him back out, because it could get too hot for Buster inside.

Although our king was busy defending his realm, chasing squirrels, and sometimes annoying visitors, his top priority was his royal family. We were Buster's most important and beloved subjects. He watched over us day and night from his perch outside our kitchen window. He seemed to sense when we were coming and going. Deb said she often saw him standing in the driveway and looking toward the road around the time the children or I were due to return home. And when we'd arrive, there was nothing he liked better than allowing us to scratch his back and pet his royal coat. He returned the adoration of his subjects with a sloppy kiss to the face, and he spent time listening to us.

He saw it as his duty to protect us. When Deb's car was parked in the driveway, he rested by the back tire as if guarding it. When we took him for walks, if any animal or person made a menacing gesture, he sprang into action. Fortunately, this rarely happened, but a few times we found ourselves struggling to restrain him with his leash to avoid a violent conflict. He reserved a particularly vicious snarl for such occasions. It announced that he was ready to fight if necessary, and we felt safer knowing that he was always vigilant in our defense. He was our king, and we loved him for it.

Vanished

*T*he years seemed to pass quickly, and by 2006, Buster had been a member of our family for twelve years. He had become a distinguished gentleman, and although he moved a bit slower, he was every bit the lovable rascal he had always been. The bonds that developed were created by our feelings for him and his feelings for us. No one could ever take that away from us.

At least that's what I thought, until one cold night in the middle of February. A few days after a big snowfall, the white powder was still piled high on either side of the road. As I drove down the driveway and approached the house, Buster ran out to greet me. He seemed a little more frisky than usual. I was coming home from a meeting in the city, and the practical side of me said his friskiness would be a problem. He would want to jump on me, and his white fur would shed on my clean, dark blue suit. Fortunately, as I got out of the car, he was distracted, and I somehow managed to dodge by him. I could tell he was disappointed as I closed the door. I felt bad about avoiding my friend, but I promised to bring him some table scraps after dinner to make amends.

We had a ritual when I brought Buster in for the night. I called him, and he came running, but he stopped just short of the door and refused to enter unless I gave him some food. Robert said I was the reason Buster was overweight. And James said that a back scratch would be more effective. But rituals are important, and we'd had this one for years. Besides, if Buster didn't eat those leftovers, I'd snack on them, and they would end up on my waistline.

I was exhausted from a long day of work and a tedious train ride home. I said hello and trudged upstairs to change into something more comfortable. It took time to decompress, and I was satisfied to eat my dinner and listen to everyone else talk about what they had done for the day. When we finished, some of us, namely I, did the dishes, and then I began my evening routine by checking to see if James had much homework. By the time I finished reading my mail and paying bills, it was getting late.

Suddenly, Deb came upstairs, looking worried. I immediately knew something was wrong.

"What is it?" I asked.

"It's Buster," Deb said, and I could tell by the tone of her voice how upset she was. "He's missing!"

I had forgotten Buster, and it was bitter cold outside. Deb had come home from an evening computer class she was taking at the high school, and he didn't come when she called. She searched by herself for a while, calling his name, but couldn't find him. That's when she came to ask for my help.

I got some leftovers out of the refrigerator and figured that food would get his attention. I went outside and whistled for Buster, but he didn't come. I walked a little farther on the driveway and tried again, but still no luck. After putting on my coat and boots, I circled the house, but he was nowhere to be found.

Starting to worry, I went back inside and confirmed Deb's news. "Buster is missing," I reported.

Robert asked, "How long has he been gone?"

James questioned, "Who saw him last and where?"

We were all milling around, getting more worried. "Everyone grab a flashlight, and let's find him," I instructed.

In a minute, a full operation was launched. We checked Buster's familiar haunts and fanned out to search the neighborhood. Deb got in her car and drove to the end of our lane and then out on the main road. Austin, my daughter's boyfriend, who was living with us until his apartment became ready, followed what he thought were Buster's tracks into the woods. Austin, a smart Texan, knew about tracking animals, so we followed him.

A large dog started barking, the neighbor's lights came on, and a voice bellowed, "Who's there?"

I yelled that we were looking for Buster, but we decided the snow was too deep and turned back.

Buster's disappearance did not seem all that unusual at the time. He escaped occasionally, but he wore a collar with his name and our phone number and fortunately always turned up by the next day. Sometimes a kindhearted driver stopped him on the road and gave us a call. One woman took him home and fed him before giving us a call. But most often, he was picked up by our town's animal control and spent the night in the shelter. We called the police and animal control, but there was no word on Buster.

The next morning, we called the shelter, hoping to hear that Buster had been found, but it had no word about Buster. The police said they had a report of a dog being spotted on a road south of our driveway, but nothing more. He had simply vanished.

Each of us tried our own approach to find Buster. The day after his disappearance was bright and sunny, so Deb spent hours driving up and down all the neighboring roads south and north of us. I tried to see if I could follow the tracks from the previous night, but I was unsuccessful. James came home after school and tramped around in the neighboring woods and called out to him. But there was no sign of Buster. We had a sinking feeling that something was different about this time, something ominous.

Unfortunately, the following day was the start of James's winter break at the high school. We had tickets to fly to Colorado for a week of skiing. But how could we leave home, knowing that Buster was still missing? The forecast for the coming week included temperatures in the single digits.

That evening, the phone rang, and it was Katie, now a management consultant living in New York. "Mom, I think you should go ahead with your trip. I'll come out for the weekend."

Deb countered, "I don't think we should go."

But Katie insisted. "Austin and I will make flyers and put them in all the mailboxes up and down the road and we can continue to search for Buster."

Deb continued. "But there might be something we could do."

Katie persisted. "Mom, there is nothing more you can do. You need a break. After I leave on Monday, Austin will continue to call the police and shelter and be at our house if Buster returns or someone calls." She reassured, "Now go and try to relax. We'll handle it and keep in touch by phone."

Fighting back the feeling that we were abandoning a family member, we packed our bags and, the next morning, headed for the airport. I said that Buster had probably been picked up by someone who hadn't noticed his tag yet, but deep down inside something told me we'd never see him again.

The following week was absolute torture. Every day, we called home to check with the police and animal shelter, but there was still no word on Buster. I thought a movie might provide a distraction, so I looked in the paper to see what was playing at the theater. The movie was *Eight Below*. Deb couldn't bear to go see this Disney film about the survival of eight huskies abandoned in the winter in Antarctica, so James went with his aunt and uncle, who were traveling with us. The movie, based on a true story, had a happy ending, but it struck a little too close to home. When they returned, James concluded it was a good thing Mom hadn't gone. It would have been too emotional for her to handle.

James was undoubtedly right. He is quite insightful, which Deb says comes naturally because "he is left-handed and sees the world differently." While hiking in the mountains with James when he was only eight years old, the two of them admired and discussed the natural surroundings. She compared the views to works of art they had enjoyed in museums. Finally, she asked him, "Do you prefer the man-made beauty of art or the beauty of nature?"

He had thought for a moment and replied, "When it comes to beauty, God wins, hands down."

On Wednesday, four days after leaving home, Deb thought of putting an ad in the newspaper. She got on the phone with the local paper back home and placed an ad to run for three days. However, we had to prepare the ad. I had my laptop computer with me, and I'm pretty handy with graphics, but I realized I didn't have a good picture of Buster. Then I remembered that my sister Sarah had visited the previous summer and had taken some beautiful photos of him. As one of Deb's friends liked to say, "Buster is drop-dead gorgeous." Well, maybe we're a little prejudiced, but after a quick e-mail to Sarah, I had a JPEG image of Buster within an hour. Sometimes big sisters are not the "crabgrass on the lawn of life," as Charlie Brown used to quip. In an hour, the ad was complete, and I e-mailed it to the newspaper. We hadn't found Buster, but at least we felt we were doing something constructive to help.

Our ad produced only one phone call on Thursday, and Austin said that the person sounded a little kooky and didn't have any information. Deb kept calling the shelter and police, but hope was beginning to fade. At twelve years of age, Buster was like an eighty-four-year-old man who had been lost in extreme conditions for a week.

As Deb and I went to sleep on Friday night, I sighed, "This is really strange. He always shows up. I wonder if he's been dognapped."

Deb shook her head. "Who would do such a thing?"

"I don't know," I replied, "but the only alternative after this long is that he's..." I couldn't bring myself to say the word "dead."

Deb knew what I meant, but she completed my sentence, saying, "Still missing." She continued, "I hope whoever has Buster is taking good care of him."

When we got home on Saturday, Buster had been missing for nine days. I had a terrible, lonely feeling as we walked into the house. Nobody said a word. I looked into the garage, where Buster should have been to greet me, and it seemed cold and empty without him. It was already dark, so our search would have to wait until Sunday.

That evening, we anxiously searched through the newspapers that had accumulated and found the ad we had placed. Our hearts sank as we saw immediately that the photo had come out too dark to be recognizable. We felt certain that was why we hadn't gotten any responses. But there was nothing we could do until the paper opened for business on Monday. We felt completely helpless. All our best efforts had been thwarted by a bad picture.

The next morning, Deb woke me at seven o'clock. "I had a dream that Buster was hit by a car and managed to drag himself to some bushes. Do you know the house down the street that's under construction?"

"Yes," I murmured.

"Well, I'm afraid that he died and is under those bushes and that's why no one has found him," she explained. "Would you go check right now? Please?."

Like a good husband, I responded, "Yes, dear." Then I put on my coat and boots and started out on the grim task of retrieving his body while hoping to avoid arrest for trespassing.

Finding nothing where Deb's dream suggested, I proceeded boldly to search several nearby properties with the prayer that everyone would be asleep early on a Sunday morning. I returned unscathed but empty-handed.

On Monday morning, Deb called the paper. They apologized profusely and agreed to rerun the advertisement at no additional cost. Deb has lots of friends, and she shared Buster's story with everyone she met. They were all on the lookout for him.

But when Wednesday rolled around, it had been almost two weeks. The only hope left for Buster seemed to be if someone had stolen him, and that disheartened us. We hoped that whoever took him would be kind, but we had a hollow feeling of unsaid goodbyes and a sense of being violated. I felt terrible that I had not greeted and praised Buster when I came home the night he vanished. It is one of those little things that you assume won't make a difference, but it did. It was an evening of despair.

Reunion

*I*t was nine o'clock on Thursday morning when Deb called me at my office. "Come quick. They've found Buster, and he's alive."

"Where?"

"Not far from here, behind a neighbor's house," she replied.

"I'm on my way." I hung up the phone and grabbed my coat. As I drove home, my emotions bounced back and forth between my heart's sense of relief that he was alive and my mind's disbelief that it could be true.

When I arrived at home, Deb and Robert met me in the driveway. Deb handed me some keys and said, "Take the minivan, and you'll need something to carry him. They said he can't walk. I've already called the animal hospital, and they are waiting for you."

Robert and I grabbed a pair of mats that kept Buster's fur and dirt off the carpet in the trunk of her car. I figured we'd improvise some way to carry him. Robert had the name, address, and phone number in case we got lost. Deb told me to look for a house down the driveway behind the big, yellow house on North Street. The last thing I remember her saying as I drove away was "Hurry!"

They said he can't walk. As I drove, Deb's words started to sink in. What did she mean by that? It was wonderful news that he had been found, but was this to be a bittersweet reunion? As I got to the road, I needed to pay attention to the traffic and find the address. I could worry about Buster's condition when there was actually something I could do about it.

Robert started to explain the events as we drove. When we arrived, Mr. Blum, a middle-aged man with dark hair and a British accent, came out and rapidly explained the rest of the story. The Blum family had been away for a week on vacation, like us. Two days ago, they had seen an animal in their ravine and thought it was a coyote. Although they had seen the ad in the paper when they returned, they didn't make the connection.

Then on this morning, their cat was pacing nervously at the kitchen window. They noticed an animal in the distance behind their house, but it wasn't moving. Their cat was so excited that Mr. Blum put on his coat and went out to investigate. Only then had he realized that it was a dog in very poor shape. He spotted the tag with our phone number and called. While he was waiting for us to arrive, he put the puzzle pieces together and surmized that this was the missing dog in the advertisement. He took out a can of cat food, which Buster ate quickly despite his weakened state.

Robert and I thanked him and started down the icy embankment with the mats in hand. In the distance at fifty yards, we could see Buster. We had to choose our footing carefully on the slippery surface. Once we got to level ground, we ran. When we got to him, Buster could barely lift his head. He was emaciated, and his once-beautiful fur was filthy with mud. He was glad to see us and tried to get up, but he couldn't move. He tried to bark, but he had lost his voice and didn't seem to have the energy to try twice. His pitiful state shocked us. I looked through the woods, and at a distance of roughly three hundred yards, I could see our house. He had been so close to making it home.

We had to move fast, as Buster appeared to be going into shock. I lifted our dog, while Robert slid the mats under him. The smell made me sick to my stomach. He had been there for a while and was lying in his own waste. Our makeshift stretcher worked fine on the level ground, but as we climbed the snowy hill, we had to stop twice as it slipped out of our hands. After reaching the top, we set him down while I opened the back door of the minivan. Mr. Blum helped us put him into the vehicle and close the door. I wanted to stop and thank him properly, but Buster was in obvious pain. I said a quick "thanks" and made a mental note to do a better job later.

It was a fifteen-minute drive to the animal hospital. I kept talking to Buster the whole way, telling him it was going to be okay and that we were almost there. Robert called Deb on his cell phone and relayed our progress.

When we arrived at the animal hospital, Robert ran in and told them we had Buster. They were expecting us and held the door while we rushed him into a waiting examination room. At that point, the veterinarian, Dr. Kramer, said it would be best if we waited in the lobby. A kindly, older gentleman with short gray hair, he had a reassuring manner. Seeing him somehow made me feel that everything would be all right. I called Deb and told her we were at the hospital and reported that Buster was safe. She said she was on her way. I paused to catch my breath and looked at my watch for the first time. It was 9:45 AM. So much had transpired in just forty-five minutes.

The next thirty minutes seemed to take forever. Deb arrived, and we waited anxiously for some word from the doctor. Finally, Dr. Kramer invited us into an empty examination room, where there was more privacy.

"Buster is in stable condition, and I think he will probably survive," he said optimistically. "It's a miracle that a dog his age could survive in such extreme cold for so long without food or water. Frankly, I am amazed." He proceeded to give us the details. "Buster has lost 20 percent of his body weight and has extensive scalding on his belly from lying in his own urine. He is extremely dehydrated and is being given liquid and nutrition intravenously. His heartbeat is weak but regular. We have given him a sedative for pain."

That was the good news, and they always give you the good news first. His demeanor changed, and I could tell there was something he was struggling to tell us.

Dr. Kramer continued. "Buster might have frostbite and will probably never walk again. During the next few days, you will have to make some tough decisions based on his quality of life."

At this point, I stopped listening.

As a nurse wheeled Buster in on a cart to see us, all that seemed to matter was that he had been found alive. Despite his sedation, he recognized us and tried to maintain eye contact, but he was clearly suffering from shock and exhaustion. As I patted his head and rubbed his back, I could feel that he was nothing but skin and bones. I kept thinking about how I had failed to praise him the night he had vanished.

Buster soon became fatigued, so we called the nurse, who came and took him back to rest in the ward where sick animals were boarded. The people at the animal hospital were wonderful to us. Although they didn't have formal visiting hours, they accommodated our trips to see Buster—sometimes twice a day. Deb sensed that he felt comfortable with the people at the animal hospital; we had boarded him there during previous vacations. Familiar sights, sounds, and smells can have a healing influence, and we were pleased that his surroundings could have a positive influence.

During that first visit by the four of us, Deb had a major insight. She noticed how Buster responded differently to each person. He gave her a look that said, "I've been through a lot, and it's comforting that you're here." Yet with me, he displayed an "I can do this" attitude. He seemed to act perky with Robert, and she could tell how much it relaxed him when James rubbed his back. As we talked among ourselves about Deb's observations, we came to the conclusion that in some ways Buster had a different personality for each of us. That was a surprising revelation about our emotional connections with him. Empathy is the ability to sense a person's emotions and respond accordingly. Some people are good at empathy while others are not, but our dog seemed to have this gift.

That evening as I lay in bed, the emotions of the day surfaced. I had suppressed them to focus on Buster's rescue. My thoughts had been practical and purposeful. The day was a blur as I looked back on it. I don't know how we managed to carry him up that icy hill. We must have been running on adrenaline. The conditions were treacherous, and yet I hardly remember thinking about our efforts; my only goal was getting him to safety and the doctor's care.

I remember being genuinely thankful that he was found alive, but as the miracle of discovery sunk in, I thought, *What's next?*

I couldn't keep the doctor's words—"never walk again"—out of my mind. How could the good news of discovery turn so quickly into feelings of despair? Never walk again? Didn't that mean we would have to put him down? How could we face that after the surge of elation from finding him?

This was when I realized the events I had just experienced spoke volumes about life. One moment, everything was wonderful, and yet things could quickly turn disastrous. Precious loved ones could be snatched away in an instant, and only then did we appreciate how dear they were to us. Our difficulties often bring these poignant moments into sharp focus.

I reached over to hold Deb, and she started to cry. I didn't have all the answers, but I knew we needed to keep hope alive.

When we went back the second day, Dr. Kramer pronounced Buster's progress "extraordinary." Buster couldn't get up on his own, but when his hind end was lifted with a sling and supported, his back legs were functioning. There was hope that he might walk again.

We were on an emotional roller coaster. First he was lost, then he was found, then he would never walk again, and then there was hope. Who knew how we would feel next?

Later that day, I began to notice things that I had missed in the rush of emotions. They had shaved Buster's front leg to insert the IV tube. I had never seen him shaved, and his skin looked eerily human. They also had removed the fur from Buster's underside, and the extent of his scalding from uric acid was now clear. But the size of the tumor on his left side shocked me. A few years ago, the vet told us that he had a tumor but advised against removing it because, with Buster's developing heart condition, "the operation to remove it would probably kill him." Its size had been masked by body fat and fur. It was bigger than a football, and since it was on one side, it made it hard for him to balance and try to walk.

The following day, Buster made little progress, and the comments about quality of life began to resurface. But on the fourth day, despite the huge tumor on his left side, Buster managed to get up on his own and walk around. He would require lots of care and rehabilitation, but he was coming home. Robert said the reason he survived was the extra body fat from the table scraps I fed him. Deb concluded that he was simply "tough as nails." Whatever the reason, Buster's amazing survival was nothing short of a miracle.

As we began to share the news, people said the newspaper should publish an article about Buster. Deb decided they were correct, and when she makes up her mind on a subject like this, it's going to happen. She suggested that I call the local paper. I phoned the *Greenwich Time* and was connected to the local news editor.

"I live in town and have a story of local interest about my dog, who survived for two weeks lost in the woods."

He responded, "People really enjoy animal stories, and this one has drama, so we would definitely be interested."

Having worked for the newspaper in my hometown, I offered, "I've drafted a short article for your consideration."

But he burst my bubble. "Thanks, but the paper does all its own writing. I'll have one of our reporters contact you, if you'll provide your telephone number."

I received a phone call to make an appointment. The next day, a casually-dressed, young reporter named Martin Cassidy and Helen Neafsey, a photographer, stopped by our house. We suggested a photo showing how skinny Buster had become, but Helen had the artistic sense to emphasize reunion, snapping a picture of Buster giving James a kiss.

Martin sat down with us at the kitchen table and asked lots of questions. Deb brought some food and invited him to have something to eat. He had a little, but newspapers have deadlines, and before we knew it, the interview was over.

The next day, with a large photo of Buster and James, the front-page headline blared: "Wayward Pooch Returns Home." The endearing picture of the two of them and the story of his survival captured the hearts of many.

Deb had a call from one of her friends. "You are not going to believe this. I was just listening to the news radio in New York, and they were carrying Buster's story," she related.

"You've got to be kidding," Deb said.

"No, I'm serious. Buster is famous!" her friend replied.

Deb called me at work to share the news. It's hard to overstate how excited and proud we were at that moment.

Katie held her new puppy Buster in her lap with a pig's ear just out of reach.

Buster dressed up as a beach bum for the costume
portion of the Dog Show.

Buster snuck a slice of pizza from the buffet.

The King struck a regal pose.
Photo by my sister, Sarah Cooper

Buster gave James a big kiss when he returned home.
Photograph by Helen Neafsey, Greenwich Time.
Southern Connecticut Newspapers, Inc., Copyright 2006

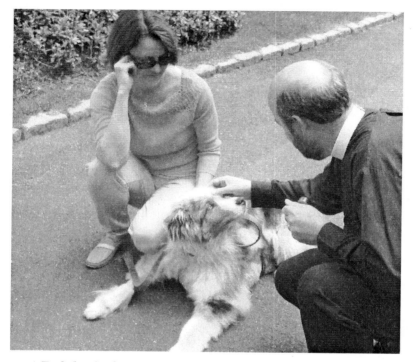

Deb looked on as Buster received a blessing from
Rev. Mark Fitzhugh.

Buster came home from the animal hospital riding
on the blue mats we used to carry him up the icy
hill where he was found.

Robert tries to give direction to Buster who was wearing one of Dad's T-shirts.

Buster smiled for the camera. Note his blue right eye and his left brown eye.

Buster ponders the meaning of life, or perhaps considers chasing a squirrel.

Hospital

*B*uster came home from the animal hospital and made slow but steady progress on the road to recovery. Since his disappearance and miraculous return a month earlier, we were very careful to keep him inside at night, particularly when the weather threatened, as it did on one rainy Sunday night in April. Around ten o'clock, James took some cans to the recycling bin in the garage and thought Buster seemed to be acting funny. James is very perceptive, and when Deb took a look, she definitely agreed that Buster was not himself. They came and asked me to take a look, too.

I found Buster downstairs in the furnace room just off the garage. It's nice and warm in there and was the perfect place for him on a cold, rainy night. But when I walked in, he didn't get up to greet me. His eyes seemed to be looking off in the distance. I tried coaxing him, but he wouldn't get up. So I lifted him and put him on his feet. He stood for a couple of seconds and then collapsed, banging his head on the floor. I was sorry I hadn't caught him in time and was quite worried about his condition.

I ran inside the house and asked Deb to phone the animal hospital immediately. During a crisis, my focus is on action. And yet, I had an unusual sense of *here we go again*. I told James and Robert to stay with Buster while I turned the minivan around so that we could load him without getting wet. By the time we had Buster in the van, Deb came back with bad news, the animal hospital was closed. My heart sank, but she explained that the recording provided the location and phone number of the Norwalk Animal Hospital in case of emergencies. This was not going to be easy. We climbed in the car and took off in the midst of a pounding rainstorm. I felt doubly nervous because I didn't know where I was going, and—more importantly—I didn't know what was happening to Buster.

Deb used her cell phone to call the animal hospital to clarify the directions and to report that we were on the way. It seemed to take forever to get to Interstate 95, but when we got on at Exit 4, we needed to go only eleven miles to Exit 15. I figured it would take ten to twelve minutes at most, but then the storm got worse. The stress was bad enough, and now it was raining so hard that I could barely see a few car lengths ahead. Fortunately, Robert was my navigator, and Deb was in back with James trying to comfort Buster. Now, Deb is a careful driver and on occasion has been known to complain about the speed of my driving. So I was surprised, and my anxiety peaked, as we neared Exit 13 and she implored, "You better speed up. I think we're losing him."

I drove as fast as conditions would allow. Luckily, the directions to the hospital were uncharacteristically clear. When we arrived, Robert ran in and soon returned with two nurses and a cart with wheels to transport Buster inside. They whisked him into the emergency room and asked us to have a seat in the waiting room. My job was to provide information and my credit card to the nurse at the registration desk so the charges could be authorized in advance.

Waiting rooms are not among my favorite places, and this particular waiting room at eleven o'clock on a rainy Sunday night seemed somewhat surreal. Since you are never going there under good circumstances, the experience feels tense and unnatural.

Once my heart stopped racing, I began to notice the surroundings. A device on a table allowed you to make individual servings of coffee or tea, and Deb decided she needed a cup of tea to calm her nerves. Finding no herbal tea, she tried the machine anyway, only to discover that it was malfunctioning. One of the nurses checked it for her and announced matter-of-factly "it does that a lot."

As I looked around, I noticed a middle-aged woman sitting by herself and decided to strike up a conversation. The television was only showing a local weather channel, and it seemed like the friendly thing to do. Perhaps some light conversation would calm my nerves. The woman explained that her dog had eaten scraps from their dinner and had become violently ill. I didn't press for details, fearing a graphic description, and told her I hoped her dog would recover quickly.

She asked about Buster, at which point Deb joined us and started to explain his story. I excused myself as Deb produced a copy of the article about Buster from the paper. The woman seemed genuinely interested, and eventually the entire night shift learned that they were treating the famous Buster Wilson.

Within half an hour, a nurse appeared and told us that it looked like Buster would recover, but they were running some lab tests. Sometime after midnight, the doctor appeared. I searched her face for clues about Buster's condition and sensed a neutral to mildly optimistic demeanor.

"Buster is fine for now," she began, "but he has suffered a significant heart attack. He has a regurgitating heart valve."

"What should we do for him?" I inquired.

I listened patiently to the medical description of his heart ailment and concluded that little short of a valve transplant would help. The doctor asked if Buster had been to see a cardiologist, suggesting one on staff or a good one in Manhattan. I didn't even know there was such a thing as an animal cardiologist and one in New York would be way out of my price range. I promised to make an appointment, but I began to wonder when letting nature run its course was better than seeking medical attention.

After paying our bill and signing the release papers, a technician brought Buster back to us, and Buster acted as if nothing had happened. Certainly, this couldn't be the same dog who only hours ago couldn't stand up. I hoped this meant his heart attack had done no permanent damage. We were all very happy and didn't seem to mind the late hour. It was almost one o'clock in the morning. Relieved, we recounted the events of the evening on our drive home. We felt his survival was a second miracle. As I fell into bed, I asked Deb if she had really thought Buster was dying on the way to the hospital. She explained that she couldn't feel his heartbeat, but it was probably because of the huge tumor on his side.

I was happy to have Buster home safely but was concerned to learn about his worsening heart condition. And I was beginning to worry about the tumor on his side. What could cause such a thing? His physical ailments were starting to get both complicated and costly. At this point, my mind was becoming numb from the stress of the evening's events. I could worry about all these things tomorrow. I looked out the window and noticed that the rain had finally stopped, and I promptly fell asleep.

Surgery

*A*fter his heart attack and trip to the hospital, Buster seemed to be stable, but he had great difficulty walking. The massive tumor on his side made him list to the left, and its bulk pushed his front leg out of its normal alignment. The doctor said that animals often get fatty tumors but rarely do they grow to such a large size. Given Buster's reduced weight and shaved underside, his tumor appeared to be huge and growing larger. I had a bad feeling about what was to come.

As summer approached, Buster's quality of life was clearly declining. It was pitiful to see him reduced to this state. His days of chasing squirrels were behind him, and now he struggled just to hobble to his familiar spots. His fur was not growing back properly, and his skin developed ulcers, which Deb lovingly cleaned with a medicinal rinse. The doctor fitted him with a plastic cone over his head so he wouldn't lick his sores. Buster must have severely damaged his vocal cords calling for help when he was lost for two weeks, and it was heart wrenching to listen to his hoarse, muffled attempts to bark.

The outpouring of emotion from our friends and the community sustained us. People were uplifted by Buster's survival story and wanted to hear how he was doing. Deb decided to write a letter to the editor as a follow-up to the news story. I encouraged her to do so, and she sent it, but their policy limited letters to three hundred words—clearly not enough space for Deb to thank everyone properly. As she put it, "Women just use more words." I was pressed into service to edit the letter, which was eventually published and well received.

Deb also decided to have a party celebrating Buster's survival. Neighbors and friends, including one pet, attended a picnic in our backyard on a bright sunny day in May. The children played in the backyard with the dogs, and then we ate all kinds of food prepared by Deb.

The group gathered for a short ceremony and a healing service at the end of the party. Deb's friend Pat read a list of witty lessons we can learn from pets. Deb was going to read a prayer, but she had forgotten to bring it with her. She ran inside while Pat was speaking, found her copy, and returned just in time. Halfway through reading the prayer, Deb discovered that she had mistakenly picked up the one to bless the altar guild instead of the one to bless animals. She was too embarrassed to stop reading, and no one seemed to notice the mix up. Afterward, she told me what had happened. "Better that mistake than reading the animal blessing to the ladies of the altar guild," I chuckled.

Buster sat in the middle of our circle and seemed to enjoy being the center of attention. He appeared to be holding court. He looked directly into the eyes of Rev. Mark Fitzhugh from our church as he received a pastoral blessing and prayers for a full recovery. It was a joyous occasion.

When Buster went in for a checkup a week later, Dr. Natalie Levitt, a smart, young veterinarian with dark hair, said that she thought the tumor was growing. His skin was stretched thin and it might never heal. I could sense her concern as we spoke. She suggested we do a biopsy to learn more about his condition, and I agreed.

A few days later, I explained the situation to the family as we sat around the kitchen table. "The doctor called today. The tissue in Buster's tumor is dead, and it looks like cancer. That's why his side won't heal." I took a breath and continued. "We have two bad choices. Buster can have surgery to remove the tumor, but with his heart condition and age, the odds of his survival are slim. The alternative is to start pain medication to keep him comfortable, and he may live a few more months."

Deb was the first to speak. "I think we have to get the cancer out of his body."

Robert added, "After everything he's survived, I think we have to give him a chance."

James was philosophical. "If I were Buster, I would rather risk surgery for a chance to live than choose a slow death."

"He's a member of our family," Deb exclaimed. "We have to try."

"Then it's settled," I concluded. "I'll call the doctor and schedule surgery."

We never considered a third choice: to have him put to sleep. After everything Buster had done to survive, we weren't going to give up without a fight.

Dr. Levitt suggested that such a delicate operation required the special surgical skill and equipment at the Norwalk Animal Hospital. Surgery was scheduled for the last week in May, but before they could proceed, Buster needed a CAT scan and a cardiology appointment.

Following these two appointments, I took Buster in for a preoperative consultation with the surgeon, Dr. Karen Cherrone. She had a warm smile and was quite earnest. As she explained the procedure, the risks involved, and what to expect, she gently stroked Buster's head and neck. The tumor was in a delicate location, with the nerves of his left leg running through it. Even if the operation was successful, he might never walk again.

As a consultant, I tend to ask lots of questions, and she impressed me with her ability to explain complex medical issues in a simple, understandable way. That gave me confidence in her abilities, but the risk that Buster might not walk again gave me great apprehension. Buster seemed to like her gentle affection, which made me feel better about our decision to proceed.

The next morning, our family bid a tearful good-bye to Buster, who we knew might not be coming back home. He clearly sensed our emotions, and James said he could see the concern in Buster's eyes.

As I drove Buster to his surgery, I remembered the first time I held him in the palm of my hand. He was so tiny, precious, and full of possibilities back then. Now he had grown old and distinguished and was facing an uncertain future. We had traveled a long road together. I had started the journey reluctantly, but over time, despite his mischief or perhaps because of it, he had won my deep affection. His relationship with each member of the family had developed at a different pace and in multiple ways over the past twelve years. But the common elements that established his vital role in our family were his humorous antics, empathy, and unconditional love.

When I dropped him off at the hospital, I gave him one last hug, and then the staff members whisked him away. He was gone, and I wasn't sure when or if I would ever see him again. Partings in these situations always feel so sudden and rushed.

The nurse said his surgery was scheduled for two o'clock in the afternoon, and they would call when it was over. The operation was supposed to last about forty-five minutes. I tried to do some work, but as three o'clock came and went, I began to get nervous. My adage is that "good news travels fast." By four o'clock, I assumed that the start of the operation had been delayed; those sorts of things always happen.

Then at four-thirty, the phone rang. It was a nurse from the hospital. The operation was not going well. Buster's blood pressure had dropped precipitously, and they were doing their best to revive him. The doctor had asked her to step out to give us a call so we would know what was going on. She said they would call again after the operation was complete.

I shared the bad news with Deb and the children, and we all began preparing for the worst. I was depressed to think that, after all he had survived, Buster was going to lose this battle. Within a half hour, the phone rang again, and the tone sounded ominous. I let it ring several times before finally answering. Dr. Cherrone was on the line. Buster had made it through surgery, but he was in critical condition in intensive care and was breathing with the help of a ventilator. He was heavily sedated, and we could not see him yet. If he made it through the night, we would be able to see him the next morning. Someone from the hospital would call later to update his status.

I hung up the phone and shared the news with the family.

Deb repeated her new mantra. "This dog is tough as nails." Then she counseled, "We have to stay positive."

As I started to calm down, I realized that I didn't know there was such a thing as a ventilator for a dog. Being who I am, I immediately wondered what such a device would cost, but decided I probably didn't want to know. For now, the only important thing was that Buster was alive.

A hospital employee called three hours later and said Buster was resting comfortably. The next morning, another staff member called to say that our dog was off the ventilator and awake. If we wanted to visit, we were welcome.

We left home immediately and when we arrived, I didn't know what to expect. I haven't spent much time inside animal hospitals, but I quickly gained respect for the skilled doctors and staff of this one. The doctor in charge was very compassionate and explained Buster's situation as he walked us in to see him.

As we came into the room, Buster recognized us, but he was unable to raise his head. He was clearly exhausted and looked dreadful. I was appalled at the sight of his blood-soaked bandage.

Deb knelt down and gently stroked Buster's head and paws. "Oh, Buster, we're here, we're here," she said in a soft, soothing voice.

I felt guilty about putting him through such a horrible ordeal. And yet, I was so relieved that he had survived. As I looked at him, I started to become concerned about his recovery.

A wave of nausea swept over me. I have always been squeamish at the sight of blood. Fortunately, there was a stool near his bed, and I sat down. I noticed two nurses nearby carefully changing the bandages on another dog. Their obvious care and skill were comforting, but the sight was not.

My attention was mercifully diverted when the doctor started to explain Buster's operation. As I focused on his story, I regained my composure. The enormous tumor they had extracted weighed ten pounds, which represented 25 percent of Buster's body weight. Just thinking about that awful, rotting mass of dead tissue within his body sickened me. The operation had gone well, until his vital signs suddenly faltered. The doctor explained that Buster had been "as close to death as you can come without actually dying." This was the part where human patients remember seeing angels and bright lights. Fortunately, they were able to revive him.

By the time we had arrived to visit, the ventilator was gone, and the bandage had already been changed twice. I couldn't imagine how the earlier ones could possibly have looked worse than the one now staring me in the face. The key to his recovery would be when and if Buster would be able to walk. He would be in intensive care for at least four days. The doctor said that the odds were not good for him to walk again, but we couldn't rule it out for a dog tough enough to go through what he had endured over the past twenty-four hours. His comments immediately prompted our story about his survival in the wilderness. Deb brought out a copy of the newspaper article, which she kept in her purse just for such occasions. It gave her confidence that he could do it again.

We had been there for nearly half an hour, and I could see that Buster was still trying to pay attention, but he was becoming fatigued. We knew it was time to go and thanked everyone involved. On the way out, the nurse at the front desk gave me a copy of his bill so far and the estimated charges for the coming day. She smiled as she asked if I preferred MasterCard or VISA. As I surrendered my card, my eye raced to the bottom of the second page to see the total. I calculated the cost per day of intensive care, multiplied by four, and suddenly it struck me, this was going to be very expensive.

I painfully remembered the day I had dismissed Deb's question about pet insurance. Then I managed to convince myself that insurance probably would have exclusions for preexisting conditions or at least limitations on most of the high-priced items like ventilators and intensive care.

Buster was a member of our family, and we were going to do whatever it took to save him. You wouldn't tell a doctor not to treat your son or daughter because of the cost. Millions of pet owners feel the same way, often spending thousands of dollars in similar situations. We loved this dog, we had made the right choice, and Buster was going to survive. At least, that's what we kept telling ourselves.

Recovery

*T*he second day we visited Buster after his operation, there was a reassuring improvement. He was able to raise his head and lick my hand. I could tell he was feeling much better. But after a while, he grew tired and laid his head down. He would need time to regain his strength, so we decided to call it a day.

Deb brought a cake, snacks, soda, and water for everyone working in the animal hospital. She appreciated the way they were taking such good care of Buster and wanted to do something special for them. With her family background in the restaurant business, food is one of her favorite ways to nurture people around her. The doctors and nurses were all pleased to have a "surprise party" and made room on a table for the spread.

The next day was nothing short of amazing. A nurse took us into a visitation room, and another staff member brought Buster walking in to see us. We were so relieved to know that he would not be crippled for the rest of his life. He walked around the room, although he soon became tired and had to lie down. He got up several times, and we could see how much easier it was for him without the gigantic tumor on his side. Deb sensed that he was hungry, which was a good sign, and asked the nurse if he could have something to eat. The nurse brought in a plate of moist dog food, which he inhaled like it was a piece of chocolate cake.

We tried to use humor throughout the ordeal to alleviate the stress, and the hospital used funny bandages to help. One time, they put a bright pink bandage on Buster. Deb teased them about using pink on a male dog, and the next day they applied a bright yellow bandage with dog bones. Experience must have taught them that colors and humor have healing benefits.

Every day we visited Buster, he got stronger. On the fifth day, the nurses removed his drainage tube and bandages. The doctor announced that Buster could come home and added some other good news: according to the biopsy, Buster's tumor was not cancerous. This was a huge relief. Apparently the tissue in the center had died and this had become a breeding ground for infection. With this terrible, decaying mass out of his body, the prognosis for recovery was greatly improved.

The doctor advised us on Buster's postoperative care. He would need to be walked four or five times a day to slowly regain his strength. His bandages would need to be changed daily, and his wound rinsed with a medicinal fluid. He was to take two different heart medications, plus baby aspirin and a diuretic to minimize fluid buildup. This was on top of the arthritis medicine he was already taking.

The doctor gave me a prescription for one of the heart medications, and I asked where I should get it filled. She told me to go to any regular pharmacy. The twenty-something pharmacist at CVS tried to keep a straight face as she entered the details into the computer. She smiled when I told her the patient's name was

Buster. When the computer prompted her to ask my relationship to the patient, I answered, "He's my dog." She giggled.

Robert and I were given final instructions when we picked him up from the hospital. Buster had to wear a plastic hood to keep him from chewing his stitches, which would be in for another week. The doctor who was releasing him suggested that Buster wear a T-shirt to protect his shaved skin from sunburn. She explained that we should tie the bottom of the shirt in a knot to keep it in place. But we must have looked perplexed, because she added, "Just ask your wife or daughter. They'll know what I am talking about."

Deb took on the role of primary caregiver once Buster came home. Each morning, she changed his T-shirt, checked his wound for infection, and administered his medications. I had an oversupply of old T-shirts that were just the right size for Buster. Putting them over his head was not too hard, but getting him to cooperate while his front legs went through the arm holes was another matter.

Then it was time to get him to take his medicine. With the occasional pill, we had always disguised it in a little piece of bread and peanut butter. But he caught on to our trick and quickly learned how to eat the part he liked and spit out the pills. The pet store solved our problem with a product called Pill Pockets. These are soft, dough-like nuggets that smell like bacon and have an open, center pocket. You drop the pills inside and roll it into a ball. Buster couldn't resist them and took his medicine like it was a treat, which was another miracle. I wonder if the company could make ones that taste like chocolate for children; but they would probably have to be sugar-free and nutritionally enhanced to attract moms' interest.

Buster's rehabilitation included walking to regain his strength and stamina, as the doctor had ordered. At first, he could go only a hundred feet. Deb was used to him pulling her, and now the roles were reversed. When he got tired, he tended to slow down, and she found herself pulling him. He had usually been willing to do as she told him, but he developed a stubborn streak after his operation. In the middle of a walk, he would simply stop, sit down, and look at her, as if to say, "I'm not going any farther." No matter how hard she tried to coax him, he was not going to move. He was acting like a stubborn, old man, which was exactly what he had become.

He looked absolutely comical in his T-shirt and plastic hood, a fact that had disguised the serious nature of his condition. The hood came off after three weeks, but the T-shirts stayed on for several more weeks. Then one day, he refused to allow me to put one on him. He nipped at my hand to let me know he was serious, and that was the end of that.

In a rather humorous instance, Robert and his girlfriend Alicia decided that Buster needed a bath later in the summer. But how could the two of them hold him still so they wouldn't get wet while they bathed him? Robert came up with the solution by attaching two leashes to Buster's collar. He lashed one to the door handle of his car and had Alicia hold the other while he did the washing. Buster looked much better after their careful grooming.

Over the summer, Buster continued to regain his strength. He had one more trip to the hospital in July due to heart problems, but the doctor adjusted his medication, and there were no further problems. His recovery period lasted a long time, but considering what he had been through, it wasn't surprising. In fact, he seemed stronger than he had been for the past couple of years. It's clear what a major burden that ten-pound tumor must have been for him.

On August 24, 2006, we celebrated his thirteenth birthday. That made him the equivalent of a ninety-one-year-old man. Given his age, he was in remarkably good shape. His fur had grown back, and he had regained his normal weight. In the morning, he once again would run out into the yard and bark to let the world know "the king" was still in charge.

His bark was a little hoarse, but it was audible, and that's what counted. He would run a little now and then, but not as fast or as far as he used to go. One morning, he even started to chase James, who was driving away from the house, but he thought better of it and came back. His hearing was not what it used to be, although I sometimes wondered if he really couldn't hear me or if he just wanted to continue enjoying his nap. Perhaps dogs have selective hearing, like some husbands.

As Thanksgiving approached, we began to reflect on the events of the past year. It had been filled with joy and sadness; hope and anxiety; good things and bad things. Buster's life was a mirror for these emotional ups and downs. His survival was amazing, and he was truly "tough as nails." He had been such a loyal dog, and fortunately, we had the opportunity to support him when he needed us. His ordeal made us realize how close we had become and how each of us had a distinct relationship with him. He was our fourth child.

As we shared Buster's story with others, similar tales about their pets spilled out, and we realized that we were not unique. The details varied, and perhaps Buster's case was a bit more extreme, but the emotional attachment that people feel for their pets is universal. Having the opportunity to share our feelings with animals is one of life's greatest rewards.

Buster's Christmas Letter

*E*ach year I write a letter which we put in our Christmas cards to update our extended family and friends on important events during the year. When we were first married, Deb and I used to write individual notes in each card, but as our network of friends expanded, that became impractical. We get dozens of similar letters in return and enjoy all the news. But what we love the most are the photo cards to see how families are growing.

The year 2006 was different. We had done lots of interesting things and passed some major milestones, providing all the basic ingredients of a good Christmas letter. But they didn't seem important when compared to the emotions we had experienced during Buster's ordeal. Given Buster's central role in our lives that year, I thought our Christmas letter should come from him. When I showed the first draft to Deb, she thought that stress had pushed me over the edge. Then, gradually, she began to warm to the idea and finally gave me her blessing and helpful suggestions. After several more drafts, Buster's Christmas letter was complete and ready to send.

Buster's Christmas Letter

By virtue of the wisdom I acquired through my amazing survival, my family asked me to write the annual letter we send in our Christmas cards. I came a little too close to that "Big Kennel in the Sky" several times this year and learned some important "dog lessons." This is a wonderful honor, and I've tried to keep my letter short and to the point. Here are my holiday lessons for pets and their families everywhere:

1) **Show your family and friends how much you care for them.** I prefer licking hands, but other gestures may work equally well for you.

2) **Take joy in the little pleasures of life.** Don't you just love chasing squirrels?

3) **Share the wonder of Christmas like you were a puppy.** Your enthusiasm and hope will help those who need it most.

I always enjoy these letters and it's great to get the newsy ones that explain the family activities. It is even better to get the photos to see how the kids and pets are growing. But what I really want to hear is how people *feel* about their family, and they seldom mention that. What is important about people and pets is not what they do, but how you *feel* about them. Here is how I feel about my family this Christmas:

Katie is the one I love because she has the kindest heart and I miss her now that she is on her own.

Robert makes me feel happy because he is always inventing funny ways to help me. He even devised a way to stay dry while giving me a bath.

James and I grew up together and he is my lifelong friend. His diplomacy and gentle way make me feel special. I only wish he was still my size.

Mom makes me feel safe and wanted by nurturing me. In fact she nurtures everyone around her. I guess that's what she does best.

Dad has always made me feel confident and secure. I appreciate the way he gives me table scraps and pays my medical bills. He always seemed to be in a hurry, but the way he greets me now makes me feel truly valued.

So how am I feeling? I am recuperating nicely and feel better than I have in years. My family loves me and I love them. At my age, I look forward to savoring every moment of 2007; I might even catch a squirrel. Hey, you never know.

I wish you and your family, including all of your pets a Merry Christmas all year long!

Best regards,

Buster Wilson

Feelings

*I*t was a hot day in the middle of May. Deb was out of town, and I had meetings in New York, so it was James who found Buster. Deb had seen him at noon, just before she left for the airport, and everything seemed normal. When James came home from school at 2:30 pm, he found Buster lying under a bush, breathing hard, and unable to move. Thinking fast and keeping calm, James rushed Buster to the animal hospital. It was a harrowing experience that James, age seventeen, will never forget.

Buster had a dangerously high temperature, and although the hospital was able to bring it down, significant damage had been done. When I arrived, the doctor said there was little more they could do for him at a regular animal hospital.

So I decided to take Buster to the Norwalk Animal Hospital. Their doctors were specialists and had saved him several times. Unfortunately, Dr. Wilde, the young veterinarian on duty, confirmed that Buster's condition was grave. There were multiple problems and no good ways to treat them simultaneously or to know what had initiated the chain of events. Even if he survived, there was little hope he would regain a normal life.

The veterinarian asked, "Do you want him revived if his heart stops?"

Without hesitation I replied, "Yes. This dog has survived so many times when we were told he wouldn't make it. I realize the odds are not in his favor, but he's part of our family." I felt a lump in my throat.

"We will do everything we can to save him." Her voice was comforting.

"Good luck," I sighed, exhausted. But as I looked into the doctor's eyes I could sense her doubt.

I called Deb to tell her what had transpired, and she planned to take the next flight home, which would not be until the next morning. Then I drove home to have dinner with James. We recounted the day's events in a quiet and subdued fashion. I kept watching the clock, knowing that each hour without a call improved Buster's chances. When there was no news as I went to bed, I felt a glimmer of hope. Perhaps Buster had confounded them again.

I was awakened when the phone rang just before midnight. It was Dr. Wilde. She told me that Buster's heart had stopped. They had managed to revive him, but they were only able to keep him alive by manually pumping his heart. She wanted to know if they should continue. I was half asleep and asked questions for several minutes, searching for a positive alternative. She patiently answered each question, but none of her responses were what I hoped to hear.

Finally, she said gently, "Mr. Wilson, I understand how attached you are to Buster, but it's time to let go."

I paused, unable to utter the words. I knew she was right, but I had no opportunity to consult my family. The awesome responsibility for Buster's fate was in my hands and mine alone. No matter how clear the medical situation, making such an irrevocable decision is gut-wrenching.

"Mr. Wilson?" she asked.

Hesitantly I replied, "It's time to let him go."

She said softly, "I know it's hard, but that's a good decision." She paused for a moment and then continued. "I'm going to put another doctor on the line so you can confirm it."

A new voice queried, "Mr. Wilson?"

"Yes, it's time to let him go." And with that, it was done.

Buster had survived many close calls and we had expected he would be with us for another Christmas or two. The winter had been mild, and although he was clearly slowing down, Buster seemed to be happy and doing well. So when the end came suddenly, it caught us by surprise, like an afternoon thunderstorm.

The next day, as James and I spoke over dinner, he said his biggest regret was that his last memory of Buster was so painful. I felt his sorrow. "It may be your last memory of Buster, but it doesn't have to be your lasting memory," I counseled.

James said that he would always remember the way Buster would rise to greet him whenever he came home. Buster was always genuinely friendly. I agreed and said that Buster made me feel special, because no matter what I was doing, he was always interested.

My fondest memory of Buster is how our feeding ritual changed over the final months. His reflexes were slower, and although he relished the treats I would toss to him, he could not always catch them. So one day, I took a treat and held it for him in the palm of my hand. He approached me and carefully took it from my hand with his tongue. I was amazed that he didn't bite me and delighted with his gentleness, so this became our new ritual. But I was left wondering if age had mellowed Buster or if I should have tried this approach long ago. The answer is probably both. This transformation provides a lesson about the opportunities for relationships to continue to develop with older loved ones as they age with dignity.

When Deb got home, she had two memories to share. She spoke first about how she had struggled with life's challenges. There were times when she would go to find Buster, put her arms around his neck, and cry. His calming eyes and gentle warmth would sooth her feelings, feelings that sometimes only Buster seemed to understand.

Then Deb retold the story of Buster and the geese. Only a week before he passed away, two geese had landed on our pond, and knowing they can be a messy nuisance, Deb tried to chase them away. When they honked back at her, Buster jumped into the pond to protect her. That scared them away, but then he looked back at her as if to say, "Oops, I'm not sure what I got myself into." She rescued him, and because he was all muddy, she gave him a bath.

Her story reminded us of the time she rescued him from the swimming pool in Milwaukee. We all laughed and told other Buster stories. That made us feel better, but we still had a sense of emptiness and sorrow. Deb said she just couldn't believe he was gone.

James comforted her by saying, "He's in a better place now, Mom." That brought a tear to her eye and put a smile on her face.

The miracle of Buster's survival and his dignity to the end are inspirations for all of us. His grace in the face of adversity touched our lives and made us realize that *feelings are more important than things.*

What a wonderful gift from a shepherd to his flock and an appropriate message as we ponder the true meaning of Christmas.